"SuperPowers delivers a real-world, concise set of practices that produce win-win-win-win relationships, regardless of success or defeat, sickness or health. Each of Matt's seven superpowers are both reasonable and achievable. Matt helps us understand and clarify how we build authentic relationships, whether the person is an employee, prospect, client, or friend.. The seven superpowers have relatable applicability to all. This is a must read and a great reference book when a little shot of positive relationology is needed."

Byron Loflin, Nasdaq Global Head of Board Engagement and founder of the Nasdaq Center for Board Excellence

"A punchy and gently challenging book to read and reflect upon for all who value genuine relationships and want to grow both individually and corporately. Matt gets to business quickly in this accessible and practical read."

Alex Fox, Law Firm Partner at Penningtons Manches Cooper LLP

"Though in practice they are rare, private banking should be about long, deep, authentic relationships. Matt entirely "gets this" – he would have been a way better banker than all of us practitioners"

Robert McIntyre, Managing Director at Barclays Private Bank

"SuperPowers is a stimulating read and timely reminder of an eternal truth that trusting relationships are not only at the core of doing good business, but also at the heart of being human. Matt is a living example of what it is to harness the 'SuperPowers' described in this book."

Mark Hews, Group Chief Executive of Ecclesiastical

"In today's inter-connected world we can easily feel overwhelmed by ever-widening circles of friends, followers and connections. In "Superpowers" Matt shares his practical, yet profound, experience and insights to help all of us make sense of our relational ecosystem and to become more effective at building authentic, meaningful relationships."

Pieter Faure, CEO of Mergon Group

"Applying the SuperPowers practices in my relationships has generated transformational improvements in my business on Wall Street. I wish I had learned and used them when I started this career 13 years ago!"

Joseph Stewart, former Vice President of Goldman Sachs, New York

"An easy to action, practical, thought stimulating, guide to take your relationship eco-system to another level."

Claudine Reid MBE, Co-Founder of PJs & Advisory Committee Chair at Lloyds Banking Group

"Finding good technical lawyers in the UK is not that difficult. Finding gifted lawyers who deliver their legal services in an emotionally intelligent way, and who develop their practices through authentic and intentional relationships, is a rarer thing. I would therefore commend "SuperPowers" to my sector, and indeed all those in business. Even small incremental improvements across the seven "superpowers" Matt explains will undoubtedly improve your individual and team performance. Relationships are the true currency of business, and Matt is an expert in helping us find the tools to authentically live that truth."

David Savage, Partner, Charles Russell Speechlys

"As a Brit working internationally I can't call Superpowers "interesting", so I will go for thought provoking. 7 key topics littered with simple (that is a compliment!) tips and tools to consider. Relationships are central to the world of work and society and those who are blessed with a long term partner know they benefit from attention and hard work. A useful guide to making new and stronger relationships, though I am intrigued to know which of Matt's circle's I am in."
Ian Hardie, Global VP Learning & Development at LVMH

"What I have enjoyed about the SuperPowers book is that it's practical and provides easy frameworks and tools to use in building powerful business relationships."
Faisal Mkhize, ABSA Bank South Africa

"SuperPowers sees Matt Bird at his best. A succinct and delightfully readable imparting of his trade secrets on the world of relationships. The what, the why, and the how... Experiential and witty, Matt gifts us the golden handbook."
Andrew Wiseman, Partner at Allens, Australia

"Matt Bird's latest book on Superpowers is exactly what the World needs right now. We need human interaction and relationships to heal divides and isolation. Since reading Relationology a few years ago I have sent copies all over the world to friends, and have followed Matt's work ever since. This book is right on time and will be the perfect follow up to growing and keeping relationships in life and business. Kindness is a Superpower!"
Matthew Welch, Head Coach at Auburn Volkswagen

"With this book, Matt has lavished on the global marketplace a gift of not only understanding the value of personal relationships but also of self-tested ways of activating a personal relationship strategy."

Boshoff Grobler, CEO of Ashburton Investments

"Every day we deal with people, those known to us or strangers. Like it or not we influence them and are gifted the opportunity to do so. In this excellent book, Matt provides seven "super powers" that show us why and how we should "treat others as we would like to be treated". In doing so, all parts of our lives flourish as we see those around us flourish. If your day involves people - this book is for you".

Andrew and Josephine Marshall,
Entrepreneurs from Adelaide, Australia

SuperPowers

PublishU Ltd

www.PublishU.com

ISBN: 9798713652579

My thanks go to
David Blakelock and Andy Kelham
whose support made this book
and much more possible.

Contents

Introduction

According to a Harvard study, the more time you spend with people, the happier you are. This conclusion followed 75 years of collecting data.

Robert Waldinger, Professor of Psychology and Director of the centre behind the research, says, "Close relationships can make or break a person's well-being. Good relationships keep us happier and healthier. Period!"

One of the reasons we are happier with good business relationships is that we grow to trust each other. If our relational ecosystem is rooted in authentic relationships, we need not worry about whether those people have our interests at heart.

This confirms my resolute belief that relationships are the true currency of business, not money. Your business will grow naturally as more people are assured that you are giving them the best service or product.

There is a fine art, or process, when it comes to building and maintaining business relationships, which I call SuperPowers. Unlike heroes in capes, however, these SuperPowers are not mystical abilities that you are born with. No, Relationology SuperPowers can be learned and should be applied in your day to day running of your business.

By applying the practice of SuperPowers, you will possess a toolbox that will help you plant and nurture your relational ecosystem, which will flourish along with your business. With more authentic and intentional relationships, you will also grow in confidence and trust.

This book contains the 7 SuperPowers that will help you embrace and work on to nurture the relationships you have, grow your relational ecosystem and generate new business from it.

Relationology SuperPowers courses are part of the Relationology Academy, which offers 100-day online courses that are proven in offering business success. To take part, you need to meet fortnightly with others in the group, but I understand that not everyone can clear their schedules for such a period of time.

So, this book, in conjunction with a package of videos, offers distance learning that any business owner can access. And for those who have taken part, it is a handy reference that you can return to as a reminder of the SuperPowers that are available to you.

SuperPower #1
Making People Feel Special

Making my way through the doors of the London hotel, I noticed a queue of delegates waiting for their name badges. Eventually, after reaching the hosts, I was handed a conference pack and, walking towards the meeting room, I began flicking through the agenda.

It was quite an early start for a conference and the schedule was indicating it was going to be a long morning. I decided that visiting the bathroom would be wise because I did not want to miss a crucial point of the proceedings to take a comfort break.

In the gents stood a man who said a brief 'hello' before launching into an unexpected grouch. His moan, it appeared, was that after a big night out the evening before, this conference was the last thing he needed, especially with such an early start. According to this unhappy chap, after viewing the agenda he had already surmised that the conference appeared tedious; worse still, he had never heard of any of the speakers. Clearly, he was somewhat miffed at having to be in attendance!

With a quick farewell, I hurried out of the bathroom and made my way to the conference room, where delegates were sitting around banqueting tables. After 30 minutes or so, the Master of Ceremonies took to the platform. After welcoming everyone and outlining the programme, the MC introduced the keynote speaker.

Rising from my table, I made my way to the platform. Looking into the audience as I made my way to the podium, I spotted among the delegates a man whose head fell into his hands! This was the same man who had earlier grumbled to me at length about the conference.

During the first break in the conference, the man from the bathroom made his way to me in the queue for coffee and said meekly, “I am so sorry. I didn’t know who you were!”

That incident has stayed with me, and I have often thought that if it matters so much to us about who someone is, then there is an authenticity problem. Should we only make people feel welcome because we know who they are?

I have a friend, Linda, who is often involved in recruitment within her business. Her task includes sifting through CVs to pick out the best candidates.

On one particular morning, she interviewed four candidates and two really stood out. The problem was there was little to separate the two, so she took the letters and CVs with the photographs attached to the front and headed down to reception.

She asked the receptionist how the two candidates had treated her on the way into the building and on the way out. Based on the receptionist’s feedback, she made her decision on the appointment.

This proves that how we treat people who we believe can do nothing for us is the ultimate test of our authenticity.

Treat everyone like a VIP

The story of the recruiter serves as a reminder that we should treat everyone equally, regardless of their perceived 'importance'. When you first meet someone you have no idea about what they do in life. You should never make assumptions, as you also have no idea who they know. Nor do you know what they will say about you and to whom.

One reason why you must treat everyone like a VIP is that you never know who they are going to become.

Professor Richard Wiseman is an expert in charisma, and he defines charisma as the impact and the effect that we have on other people, and how they feel after encountering us. He goes on to explain that 50 per cent of charisma is innate: we're born with a particular charisma, but half of it is learned and developed.

Taking part in this Relationology SuperPowers course is about developing and learning a particular charisma that makes other people feel special. So let me ask you some questions:

- If a person has a very high opinion of themselves and a low view of others, how do they come across to others?
- How might you describe their behaviour?
- What words come to mind when you meet someone like that?

You might say they are arrogant, self-serving and selfish.

In contrast, what would you call someone who has a very low view of themselves but a high view of others? You might describe them as insecure, intimidated or believe they have low self-esteem.

What about those who have neither a high view of themselves or other people; they may have a low view of who they are and of others. You may consider them as timid or even depressed.

How do you describe someone with a very high view of others and an equally high view of themselves? These people are usually confident, courageous, bold and comfortable in their own skin. As a professional, you should belong to that group of people, but we all have bad days when another part of our charisma might be on show.

Your place of regression

Where do you regress to in a bad moment? Do you blame others and look down on them? Or do you feel like everyone else is perfect, so you feel intimidated or insecure?

We all have days or seasons in life when things appear to be going against us. And our feelings in those times are reflected in our dealings with others. When you face difficulties you usually show your true colours, which is the part of charisma that Professor Wiseman would say is the innate half. As a result, you treat others as anything but VIPs; so it is in these times of regression that you must work harder to make people feel special.

Learning strategies to bounce back when things go wrong is important in developing your personal resilience. Once you know how to recalibrate, you rebound much stronger and become more confident. Even in tougher times, you will become most like yourself if you learn the procedure.

If, like me, you constantly blame yourself when things go wrong, you can end up feeling intimidated and insecure, which is reflected in how you approach others. I have had to learn that I need to demonstrate confidence at all times, and this has helped me in winning others over.

So, what is your place of regression? Why do you go there? How does it make you and others feel?

Be determined to work on the 50 per cent of your charisma that is learned and developed through life experience. And there are lots of ways of doing this.

Developing charisma

“Listen with your eyes” is something that I encourage my children to do. This isn’t a contortionist’s act, but a simple rule, which is to look at someone when you speak to them. In my book Relationology 101, there is a chapter called ‘Don’t Open a Shop Unless You Know How to Smile’. No matter what business you are in, it is so important to smile because it helps people feel comfortable, relaxed and special.

Easing people into a conversation is also an important skill and something charismatic people are experts in. ßAsking someone how they are allows the conversation to be focused on the other person; they will relish the opportunity to talk about themselves.

The next part of your strategy is to listen! For me, listening is a gift. Asking a question and keeping quiet allows your time and attention to be focused on the other person. Most people are desperate to talk about themselves and to share what is going on in their lives, so be ready to listen.

It can be easy for your mind to wander when someone is intently sharing their thoughts and feelings; so make sure you are completely present, listening to them attentively. You should be heartfelt, genuine and authentic when spending time with people.

Remember, you are not networking, which is where people are in it only for what they can get out. As a Relationologist, you should be investing in relationships and building and growing them through the experience.

All these practical strategies help you make people feel special.

MAKING PEOPLE FEEL SPECIAL

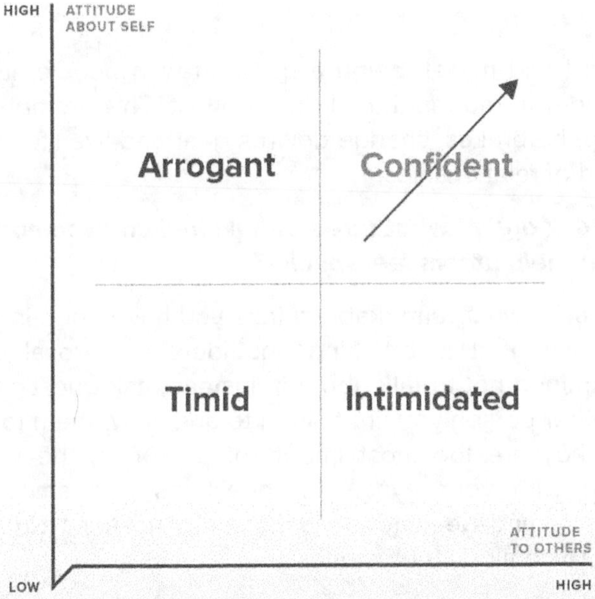

Matt's Mission

I want to offer you a challenge: What three practical things, or behaviours, could you adopt to help make other people feel more special in your company?

It doesn't matter whether the other person is a waiter, bus driver or a receptionist! But what can you do to make them feel special?

When I find myself being a bit short with people, it is a reminder to me that I am living too fast. This prompts me to tap the brakes, change down a gear and live life at the speed of relationships.

So, I ask again, what three behaviours can you commit to that help others feel special?

No matter what remarkable things you have done in your life, even if it is brushing shoulders with royalty, be determined not to talk about it. Instead, ask questions of the other person you are talking to and allow them to feel that they are the most important person in the world. Listen with your eyes, ask questions and smile. Be attentive and be ready to ask other questions to allow them to continue their stories.

When they leave your company, they will feel so important that they will remember you as the person who made them feel like a VIP.

SuperPower #2 Keeping In Contact With Everyone You Know

It was rather exciting receiving an invitation to be a panellist at an event being organised by the Harvard Business Review. After a lively and fascinating session with lots of questions about how best to run and grow businesses, the Editor asked if they could have a word with me.

They wanted to know if I would like to write an article about an issue a lot of readers had asked the magazine to address: the difficulty keeping in contact with people as you go through your career.

This is a topic that I already knew a lot about, but I relished the opportunity to research the matter in further detail. And I wasn't disappointed!

After some digging, I found the results of a survey from online business platform LinkedIn during my studies. They had polled their users and discovered that:

- Some 38 per cent of people found it immensely difficult to keep in contact with people
- A total of 49 per cent said the biggest problem with keeping in touch was the pressure on time
- And 79 per cent of respondents agreed that relationships were critical to their well-being and careers

It's staggering that while we are aware that relationships are central to our happiness, the practice of keeping in touch with those relationships puts us under such great pressure.

Your relational ecosystem

Business relationships are not just something I help people with, I have rather a large number of them myself. As well as Relationology International, I am involved with a number of other enterprises. At the heart of each are the relationships that make them tick, and one of my functions is as a connector of people.

So, as you can imagine, it means I have an enormous number of relationships to manage. I call this my relational ecosystem! You have one, too, and like any ecosystem, it requires regular investing in and tending to to ensure it is healthy.

I see the ecosystem as five concentric circles: at the very central circle are the relationships that are central to my life, and I call these my soulmates.

Soulmate circle

These are the people that I can talk to about anything and everything. You could choose a number of people to be a soulmate, but the reality is you can't share life at that level with lots of people. It would be far too exhausting!

Most of us have fewer than five people we choose to be soulmates with. An engaging academic paper, called A

New Look at Social Support, identified two roles that close relationships have in our lives.

During times of adversity, difficulty and challenge, those close 'soulmate' relationships are sources of strength, it said. They become a place where we find solace, comfort, reassurance and encouragement; they are a safe place to be.

Such relationships also have a function during times of opportunity, and the paper's authors called these relational catalysts. They are the people we dream with and imagine the future with; we bounce ideas around and problem solve with them. Together, we create and innovate with those people and can go out into the world with courage and confidence and boldness.

For me, my soulmates are both sources of strength during times of challenge and relational catalysts during times of opportunity.

Super-family circle

The second circle is what I call my super-family. This includes my immediate family, of course, but also includes a cluster of people who are virtually family to me. There are probably no more than 15 people within this circle; and I am so close to them that they feel like family.

Speed dial circle

Next, is the third circle, which is my speed dial circle. On my smartphone there is an allocation for 50 speed dial numbers. Those numbers belong to the people I speak to most weeks. They are also the people who often receive pocket calls from me when I accidentally press the speed dial button!

Such relationships make my world go round at both a personal and professional level. Without them, I wouldn't be able to be who I am and do what I do.

Social relationships

Within the fourth circle are the people who belong to my social relationships circle. I know their names, know their families and what they are passionate about.

Professor Robin Dunbar, an Oxford University anthropologist, studied the cognitive capacity for human relationships. He calculated that our average is 150, and this is known as Dunbar's number.

Now, if you are an introvert you are probably reading this and thinking, "My goodness, I don't know 150 people!" If you are an extrovert, however, you are probably stunned the figure is so low, as you have the cognitive capacity for more than 150. Remember, that Dunbar's number is an average!

I have a list of relationships and once a month, I will read down the list. In doing so it prompts me to reach out to someone. To those people I have been in contact with for some time I will send them a note, give them a call or arrange a get-together. It really helps me keep my focus because this is the one circle in my ecosystem that, when I'm under pressure, gets pushed out a little bit.

Social media circle

The final circle is entitled my social media circle. We can all have thousands of people that we keep in contact with via social media circles. It's just such an incredible gift.

Within this circle are people that we do not necessarily know. We know their name and may have met them once or twice or never. I have a friend in my social media circle who I knew 20 years ago and then they moved to a different country.

Although we've moved on in life and lost touch, we have reconnected thanks to social media. We are now looking at doing some work together, and this was all possible thanks to social media.

You can't be friends with everyone

The relational ecosystem circles work for me because they help me differentiate my relationships. I would like to encourage you to recognise the value of being able to distinguish between relationships because it is impossible to be friends with everyone. But don't forget that even though you can't be friends, you can be friendly with everyone!

To differentiate your relationships, I find that using the Pareto principle helps. This principle, if you are not aware of it, states that around 80 per cent of consequences, or outputs, come from 20 per cent of causes, or inputs.

This principle could be applied across different enterprises that I have worked with. Normally, 80 per cent of revenue comes from 20 per cent of clients. And it's a rule of thumb that applies in so many different contexts. In the Harvard article, I recommended applying the Pareto principle to our relationships.

Networkers put 100 per cent into only the relationships they get something from. My belief is that you should stop networking and start relationships. It is important, therefore, not only to invest in relationships you get something from, but also to be generous and give a bit of yourself to others you don't.

So, by applying the Pareto principle, I believe that 80 per cent of your time, energy and resources should be used into the 20 per cent of your relationships that produce 80 per cent of the results in your work.

The most transparent businesses that differentiate customers that I can think of are airlines. I usually spend a lot of time on British Airways flights.

When I first started flying, I was just a customer that they looked after. As I flew more, I received a bronze card, then a silver one before graduating to a gold card. As a loyal frequent flyer, you become one of their 20 per cent of customers that qualify for additional benefits. The airline invests more time and energy resources into you.

Instead of arriving at the airport and seeing a whole lot of queues, you step behind a screen where there are a lot of extra desks, which means you check your bags in more quickly.

There are hardly any queues once you reach security and then you move straight into a lounge, where you can drink champagne and enjoy hot food. You can even take advantage of a little massage if you're on a long-haul flight; and you can take extra baggage on board and access other benefits.

Airlines differentiate their customers because they recognise that 20 per cent of customers produce 80 per cent of their revenue.

Charities do the same thing and all businesses that are smart differentiate their relationships because they recognise you can't have the same relationship with everyone you know.

How do you keep in contact with people? How do you keep in contact with everyone? It has to be through differentiating relationships.

Matt's Mission

The challenge, should you choose to accept it, is create your own relational ecosystem. You can take as much or as little of my five-circle model as you'd like, or you can make up your own.

But what's really important, once you've segmented your relationships and differentiated them, is to work out what you commit to each of them.

For example, one of my commitments is that I contact anyone within my relational ecosystem on their birthday when social media platforms alert me to them. Even if it's somebody I haven't seen for years, I would always wish them happy birthday and send a message.

So, I want you to think about the service level that you commit to for each part of your ecosystem. I commit to sending birthday messages to those in my social media and social relationships circles. For those I have the closest relationships with, I look down my list to see if I am prompted to reach out to them in some way.

As for those in my speed dial circle, I sometimes flip through my phone to see if I have forgotten something that I can contact them about. My super-family and my soulmates are the people that I commit to share a meal with on a regular basis.

My challenge to you is to create your own relational ecosystem.

I would encourage you to draw your ecosystem and write down the service level you agree to for each circle, or each aspect, and send it through to me. I'd love to see your ideas and I promise to get back to you with a few thoughts of my own.

By putting this strategy in place, you will soon be contacting more people than you ever have managed before.

KEEPING IN CONTACT WITH EVERYONE

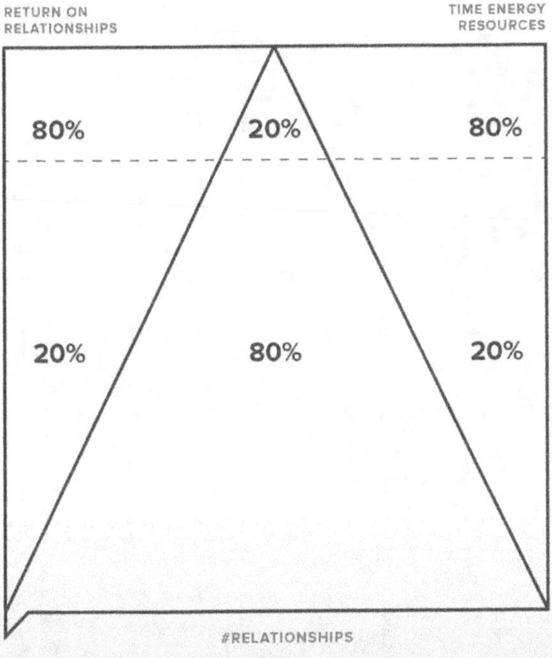

SuperPower #3
Generating New Business

After being used as an external consultant for a number of years for a professional services firm, I was somewhat surprised when the partner I worked with announced his retirement. Of course, I congratulated him and he rather excitedly spoke about his plans... they certainly didn't involve slowing down!

As we chatted, I pondered the future and wondered how my relationship with the client would continue as I was losing such a close connection within the firm.

I decided to ask him directly, "What will happen with future work here when you have retired?"

The retiring partner suggested that I should arrange a fine wine and artisan cheese event. Now, this wasn't as random an idea as it sounds because, as a wine and cheese connoisseur, I regularly organise such events.

He suggested I should cover the cost of an evening and he would invite a dozen partners along who he thought I should get to know.

We had a great evening, splitting into two teams and competing together to taste the wines and pick the cheeses we thought went best with the wine. It was great fun.

At the end of the night, I explained that I ran a business consultancy helping leaders and their businesses build rewarding relationships. I then handed everyone a goody bag of cheeses and a copy of my book, Relationology 101.

Over time, I began to meet regularly with one of the partners who was at the cheese and wine event. During one lunch meeting, he mentioned that he had just been promoted and was looking after some of the partners running the biggest global accounts.

“Technically they are brilliant,” he said, “but they often tell me that they want help with client relationships.”

He then moved from this comment and asked me whether I could design a Relationology programme to help strengthen their relational capability. As you can imagine, I said I would be delighted to help – and it came about thanks to a relationship. That, in my view, is how all new business opportunities come about – through relationships!

In 1974, Professor Mark Granovetter, from Stanford University, conducted research which showed that 56 per cent of people found their jobs through a relationship.

Granovetter went on to publish a famous paper called ‘The Strength of Weak Ties and in it he concluded if we only build relationships with people like us, we limit our access to jobs and opportunities that people like us are in. If we build relationships with people unlike us, however, we have access to the jobs and opportunities that people unlike us have. So, if you're hungry for opportunity, for promotion or a new thing, don't just build any relationship: build diverse relationships.

Diversity is something I want to look at later. First of all, I want to focus on the way that relationships create opportunities for us.

Relationships and jobs

Sometimes I work in the recruitment industry helping recruiters build effective relationships with candidates and clients alike. It is commonly thought that two-thirds of jobs are never advertised. They never go to recruitment firms because they're given to people already known by the employer. If you are running a business, particularly a small business, recruiting somebody on the basis of an application letter, CV, an interview and a couple of references is high risk.

The safest route is to hire someone we know can do a good job because they've done it for us somewhere before. It makes more sense to employ somebody who we trust and the only way to do that is through the relationships we know.

If you're looking for a job and checking recruitment sites and advertising, you are only looking at one-third of jobs that are available.

Relationships are what open opportunities for us; they create new jobs, contracts, relationships and business leaders.

Five steps to new business

I use five very practical strategies for generating new business and new relationships. The strategies are like the five rungs of a ladder.

1. Self-introduction

A friend of mine runs a film-making business, and he helps organisations capture the essence of who they are and what they do in a short film. It's just brilliant.

He was working at home one day at the kitchen table when Mother Nature called, so he went off to the bathroom. As he sat there, he found that his wife had left a pile of magazines for just such an occasion. He picked the first magazine from the top of the pile. It was actually a brochure for a clothing brand and as he looked at the incredible pictures, he thought, "Wow, if they could do the same print, imagine what they could do on film."

After heading back to his kitchen table, my friend Googled the name of the chief executive of the business. He managed to find out his email address and sent him a note to recall the events from earlier in the day. A few days later he was invited to meet with the chief executive of that business and started a relationship. As a result, they worked together to make numerous films for that organisation.

I remember reading the London Evening Standard and an interview with the incoming chief executive of a bank. It was a fascinating read and in the interview they mentioned something that he and I had in common. At that moment, I decided I would like to meet the man himself. I decided to write a letter to him to congratulate him on his appointment and I mentioned the interest that we had in common and offered to take him out for a drink.

Amazingly, he very generously accepted and we started a relationship. He has since moved upwards in his career and done some amazing things; at the same time, he has become a good friend to me. He's one of my mentors and his family foundation helps fund the NGO that I lead, Cinnamon Network International. But it all came about through a self-introduction.

Now, for every story of great success, I can tell you dozens of stories of the door being slammed in my face or probably just their introduction. Self-introduction completely ignores the high risk of rejection, but when it works it can be really powerful.

2. Facilitated introduction

I describe the facilitated introduction as 'de-risked' self-introduction because you get someone who knows you and the person you want to meet to facilitate an introduction. There is a transfer of trust between the introducer and you because they trust the introducer. As a result they will begin to trust you enough to get the door open.

This is actually what I wrote about earlier, about the partner who suggested I should host a cheese and wine event. If I had invited them myself, I doubt anyone would have turned up. But because they trusted the retiring partner, they trusted me and the event and turned up. That is the power of the facilitated introduction.

3. Client recommendation

When it comes to client recommendations, you are unlikely to know that they are taking place. Someone who has used your services will tell another person about you during a chat. This all goes on in the background, but beware that this conversation can be negative as well as positive! If you've done a bad job for someone the discussion might not be a recommendation at all.

During lockdown in 2020, I did a piece of work for a company that went very well. A couple of months later, someone reached out to me and said, “Matt, you were recommended to me – could we have a conversation?”

That happened and it led to new work, which shows how powerful client recommendations can be. Sometimes it leads to immediate business, sometimes the initial contact may not result in business for some time. But those connections are very helpful and I encourage you not to lose touch in those instances.

4. Targeted referrals

Targetted referrals are like gold! These are when someone has a need for your services and someone refers you to that person at their point of need. It’s not an introduction or a recommendation, it is a referral for business.

At the end of all the Relationology Academy courses, I ask people if they would be happy to make a targeted referral. I ask if there is anyone they know who might benefit from what they've just experienced on my programme.

Very often, when those who take part make those referrals, the person they refer ends up buying a place on the next course.

5. Brand advocates

The advocates of your brand are not always clients of your business, but they love what you do. They will go out there and tell other people – they are like evangelists for the cause.

I'm an Apple user; I have an Apple Watch, Apple iPhone, Apple Tablet, Apple MacBook – basically I'm a fan. Somehow, Apple manages to engage their customers and make them passionate fans.

There are all sorts of products and services that people become an advocate for. People get very passionate and become brand advocates – whether that is for Uber, a clothing brand or a particular TV channel or radio station.

These are the five strategies I implement and I rank them in order. At the bottom are the low cost ones. Making a self-introduction costs you nothing, whereas building targeted referrals and brand advocates costs a lot of time and money and continuous care for people.

While the strategies at the bottom of the ladder are low cost, they are higher high risk, high risk of rejection that is! You are much more likely to get turned away by a self-introduction than you are a facilitated introduction.

This is how I generate new business and create opportunities and it can work for your organisation too.

In a sense, each strategy is represented by LinkedIn. The self-introduction on LinkedIn is writing and introducing yourself to someone and asking them if they'll accept you as a connection.

Facilitated introductions are where you ask somebody who knows the person you want to meet. You may see that the person you want to meet is a 2nd or 3rd connection of someone who is your 1st connection. Through LinkedIn, you can ask them if they'll facilitate an introduction.

Then you've got recommendations on LinkedIn; they call these testimonials. You can ask a connection if they would be willing to write a testimonial about the value of what you have done for them.

Using LinkedIn allows you to post that you want to offer opportunities or ask if anyone can connect you to someone who can help you. This is a target referral.

And then the brand advocates recommend you. This has happened to me, where I received a sudden notification to say my name had been mentioned in a conversation thread. It was someone I know quite well who raved about my services. Their company has previously used my services, and as they were already advocates of my brand they were more than happy to 'evangelise' about them!

The business ladder, as I've called it, actually parallels with the strategies used on a platform such as LinkedIn.

Which of these strategies do you use the most? Which of them do you use the least and which of them do you think you could use to great effect?

GENERATING NEW BUSINESS

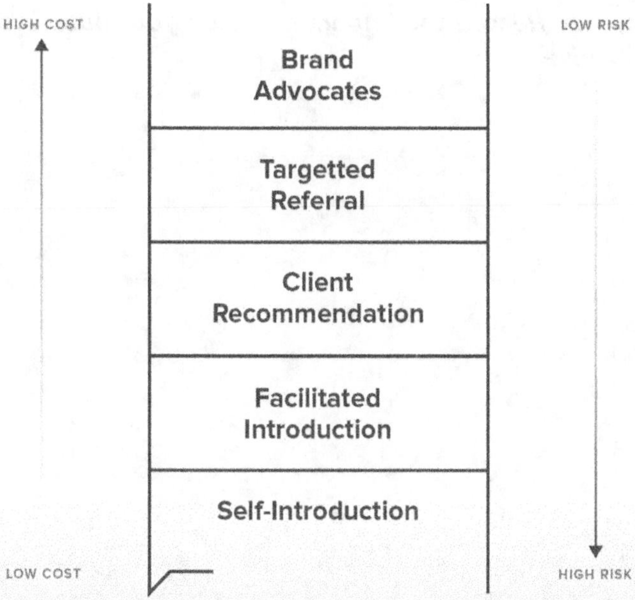

Matt's Mission

The challenge, should you choose to accept it, is to adopt and intentionally use one of these strategies. Choose one you don't normally use as this SuperPower is all about generating new business opportunities.

Begin to use it, use it three times and see what happens. Record the impact it has on your business or enterprise.

SuperPower #4
Developing Diversity

Adjusting the jacket of my best suit and ensuring my pocket square was perfect before leaving the house, I was getting excited about the momentous event I was heading to. My destination was Westminster and the event was extremely important: the bicentenary of the abolition of the transatlantic slave trade.

I was privileged to be invited to such a special occasion, where the Prime Minister would be a special guest. After the main event, attendees were invited to a drinks reception, where across the room I spotted a gentleman of Afro-Caribbean descent. His snazzy dress sense was as noticeable as mine!

Making a beeline for each other, we started a conversation and after an enjoyable chat, we decided that we should arrange another meeting. Instead of a traditional lunch or coffee, I invited him on a shopping trip.

Our destination was my favourite tie shop in London's West End, where the brightly dressed chap purchased what he now calls his 'Matt Bird set' of tie and pocket square.

While we were enjoying each other's company and encouraging each other over our dress sense, we realised that the Afro-Caribbean gentleman and the quintessential Englishman came from two very different worlds. So we agreed that I would introduce him to my world and he would introduce me to his. This is where our journey began!

If I am being brutally honest, I learned more about myself than I learned about him over time. One of the things I learned is that prejudice is something we learn; we are not born with prejudice!

There were days in this relationship when my equally dapper counterpart would turn up for our meetings anywhere between half-an-hour to an hour late! On one occasion, he even cancelled at the last minute.

Rather than understanding the issues he was facing, I simply stereotyped him and dismissed his poor timekeeping as being a typically laidback approach in his community.

As we got to know each other in the years that followed, he told me why he was regularly delayed. I realised, as he shared his personal situation, that I was being prejudiced in my thinking and stereotyping of his lack of punctuality.

He quietly told me what a member of his family was facing. It was an extremely challenging time for him.

Back in the early days I didn't know that. I fell into the trap of forming prejudices in my own mind about people like him, rather than understanding his individual circumstances. As I got to know him, my prejudices began to decrease.

As we truly get to know people and understand them, any prejudices we may have disappear. We see through those things as we get to know the intricate details of the real person behind the facade!

What I discovered was that part of the ethnic community, of which this man is a part, is overrepresented in our criminal justice system. And this is not marginally, it is significantly.

His community is also overrepresented in suffering from a number of critical health conditions. And it is also overrepresented in low paid jobs or no employment.

One area in which his community is underrepresented is at an executive level of business, media and politics – in fact almost every other sector. Yes, there are always notable exceptions, but they are just that... exceptions!

Snowy Peak Syndrome

I remember reading an article in The Guardian which was headlined 'The Snowy Peak Syndrome'. The writer explained that within the foothills of British society, there is lots of diversity. But, they wrote, as you ascend the mountain and reach the peaks of executive leadership there is always an absolute whitewash.

Diversity and inclusion are often described thus: diversity is being invited to the party, inclusion is about being asked to dance. But diversity and inclusion are not just the right thing, they are also the smart thing. The same can be said of pursuing racial and gender equality.

I call this IP...

***I** is for innovation!*

Putting a group of people from different backgrounds, experiences and education into a room to solve a problem will result in abundantly creative solutions. But putting a group of people who have been educated in an identical way and grown up within similar communities will culminate in the same solution time and again. You see, diversity in relationships drives innovation.

Consulting group Hewlett Consulting revealed the results of research around innovation and diversity in a Harvard Business Review article. Their work showed that diversity always resulted in greater innovation.

The report also highlighted two-dimensional diversity. The first dimension is inherent in which the authors described diversity as being where we are born, our culture and language we speak. There is also acquired diversity, which is acquired through our education and experiences in life along with many other developmental factors.

What the researchers discovered was that companies with two-dimensional diversity out-innovate and out-perform others. These companies' employees are 45 per cent more likely to report that their firm's market share grew over the previous year and 70 per cent more likely to report that the firm captured a new market.

What great indicators of innovation! I believe that diversity in relationships isn't just the right thing to do, but it's the smart thing to do because inclusion drives innovation.

***P** for performance*

McKinsey is the world leader in strategy consulting and have published a report, called 'Delivery Through Diversity', which they update regularly. Looking at the profitability of businesses, the authors say that diverse executive teams help increase the likelihood of profitability by 27 per cent.

In the previous SuperPower I quoted Professor Mark Granovetter, whose research showed that 56 per cent of people found their jobs through their human connections. Professor Granovetter went on to write a very significant paper called 'The Strength of Weak Ties'. Psychologists refer to weak ties as acquaintance-based relationships, whereas strong ties are our closest relationships and friends.

Granovetter argues in his paper that there is strength in those weak ties, advocating the power of acquaintance-based relationships. The fact is that like attracts like, so you tend to build relationships with people like you because it's easiest. They could be those who share your hobbies, people you work with or those who went to school with you.

Building relationships with people unlike you is a lot more difficult because there are other obstacles to overcome on the journey. You see, we all tend to build homogeneous relationships, relationships with people that are like us rather than heterogeneous relationships, those unlike us.

If you only build relationships with people who are like you, you will only have access to the opportunities that people like you have. Whereas, building relationships with people who are unlike you will help you access opportunities that people unlike you have.

This is an essential lesson because to increase opportunities in life, you need to build diverse and inclusive relationships. Crucial to this is building some relationships with people who are unlike you. Psychologists refer to these as bridging relationships because they help you bridge from one culture, sector or market.

What I discovered with my Afro-Caribbean friend is that he helped me bridge my relationships into a whole new world that I would never have discovered. And that a bridging relationship with him transformed over time to become a bonding relationship.

How diverse are your relationships?

My developing diversity model is a Venn diagram with overlapping circles. And in it, I'd like to ask you: How diverse are the ethnicities, ages and genders of your relationships?

There's a fourth circle in the Venn diagram that I have titled 'other', and you can put in there whatever other aspect of diversity is important to you.

You may want diversity in the geographic location of your relationships. Do you need more relationships in the north or south, perhaps in other countries, perhaps in other continents?

Do you need to develop relationships in different markets or in different sectors? There are so many diversity challenges and opportunities that each of us face.

Consider where you are strongest in your diversity and also which area of diversity could most benefit from your time and attention.

Matt's Mission

My challenge for this SuperPower, should you wish to accept it, is what I call the salt and pepper challenge.

I would like you to start or strengthen one relationship with someone who is very unlike you.

This is not just an exercise, it requires 100 per cent commitment otherwise it has no authenticity. See what happens, and then over months, years, even decades, that relationship could become as transformative for you as mine has been for me.

Do you need to develop relationships in different markets [illegible] different sectors? There are so many diverse [illegible] challenges and opportunities that each of us face.

Consider where you are strongest in [illegible] diversity [illegible] areas of diversity need most urgently your time and attention.

Matt's Mission

My challenge to you this [illegible]—should you wish to [illegible] is [illegible] the [illegible]

[illegible]

[illegible]

DEVELOPING
DIVERSITY

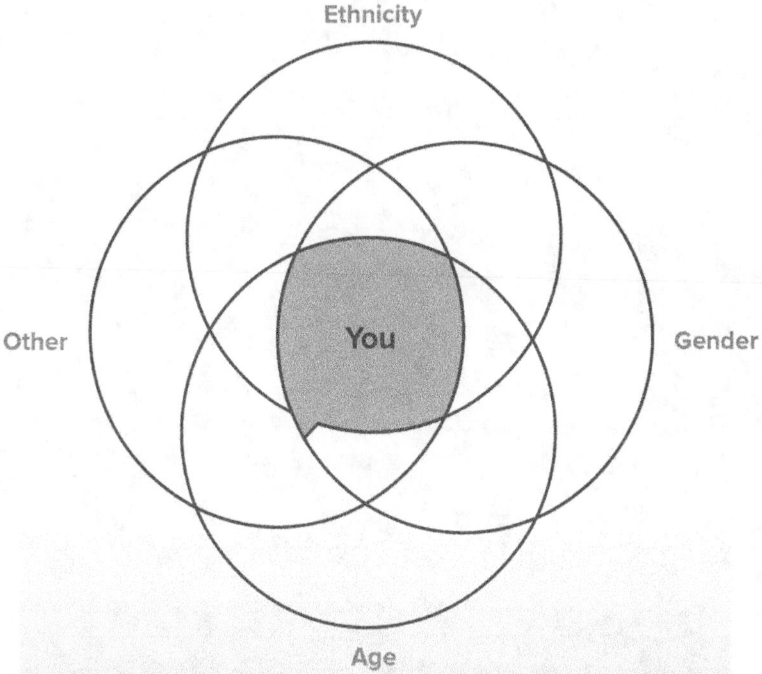

SuperPower #5
Leading High-Performance Teams

My daughter loves clothes and fashion. Matilda enjoys nothing better than picking different items and making great outfits out of them. She loves to take me shopping, and I'm convinced it's because of my great company and conversation. My wife, on the other hand, thinks it's because of my wallet!

Either way, I am very happy to take her out for the day and pay as we hit London's West End shops. It is quite an experience for me.

The first time we went on one of our shopping expeditions, I was somewhat taken aback when we went to pay for clothing. It wasn't the price, but the fact that the shop didn't sell clothing in sizes. When I enquired about this, Matilda replied, "Daddy, they only have one size in the whole of the shop!"

As I looked around, I noticed that the shoppers were of a similar age and a similar profile. One size really does fit all when it comes to this clothing brand!

When it comes to leadership and leading high-performance teams, however, one size never fits all. The best leaders in the world are able to read other people and, importantly, regulate themselves in order to get the best possible outcome.

For me, there are two principles in leadership: knowing how to lead yourself, and knowing how to lead people. It is about self and social awareness; about understanding the way that we and others are hardwired. Learning to recognise this helps get the best possible outcome in the relationships you form and the teams you build. As a result, those teams are able to deliver the best performance.

Building teams has become more challenging because working from home has become the new normal. When we work from home we are more inclined to do things in our own way and not that of the collective office environment. Finding our own unique ways of working, personal preferences have become more prominent.

The concept of preference

If you were to pick up a pen to write your name on a piece of paper, how long would it take you? I would imagine your answer is that it wouldn't take long because you do not have to concentrate much to do so.

But what if I invited you to put your pen in the other hand and write your name on the same piece of paper? How would you find that experience? Well, the result probably wouldn't be as good. It would take you longer and you would need a lot of very focused concentration. Surprisingly, such a simple task would also be energy draining. The reason for a straightforward exercise to be such a challenge is because it is not your preference.

Over the years, I have developed an understanding of the different preferences people have. Each person has a unique profile of who they are and the way they like to do things.

I have developed six preference profiles to help you understand who you are and the category the people you are leading identify with.

'Introverts' and 'Extroverts'

First, I would like to ask: Are you introverted or extroverted? Now, often introversion and extroversion are misunderstood. It's nothing to do with how you arrive and behave at a party because 'Introverts' can, in fact, be quite amazing at parties. The difference is that an 'Introvert' will leave a party exhausted and craving some personal space while an 'Extrovert' will be energised and ready for more.

'Introverts' are stimulated through their internal environment, predominantly, and 'Extroverts' are stimulated by the external environment.

'Logical' or 'Creative'?

The second preference pair classifies people who are left brain dominant and people who are right brain dominant.

Those who are left brain dominant are logical, analytical, and rational. These are the people who love to communicate by using spreadsheets. Individuals who are right brain dominant are creative, innovative, and enterprising. They constantly come up with new ideas and they have great creative expression.

How I remember the difference is that L stands for Left brain and also for Logic! And the R stands for Right brain and also for the R in cReative.

'Project People' and 'People People'

'Project People' hate to be interrupted when they're in the middle of something. It doesn't matter what's happening, they would rather put off a conversation until they get the job done. This group is very focused on completing the task and project.

'People People', on the other hand, will always stop if somebody needs their help and are more than happy to be interrupted by someone.

On the downside you could view 'People People' as getting easily distracted, while 'Project People' can leave 'casualties' along the way because their determination to get things done can leave others feeling like they're not being listened to or understood.

No matter what category you believe you belong to, there are advantages and disadvantages of being one or the other.

'Early Bird' or 'Last Minute.com'

When it comes to your schedule, do you think, "I'll work on that when it's due", or do you plan your work weeks in advance? Are you happy to ask someone to call tomorrow to discuss something, or do you prefer to schedule a call two or three weeks ahead?

The 'Early Bird' will schedule their holidays while the hectic 'Last Minute.com' person will spontaneously book a trip for the following week. They will also pack their suitcase almost as they're walking out of the door to the taxi, while the 'Early Bird' had their case packed days ago.

Dealing with and approaching each person requires consideration to ensure you don't make an 'Early Bird' panic or the 'Last Minute.com' person feel constrained.

'Owls' or 'Larks'?

The fifth preference I use when trying to understand people is to ascertain whether they are 'Owls' or 'Larks'. 'Owls' are people who love to stay up in the night, they come alive as the sun goes down.

I have friends who are 'Larks' and are at their very best first thing in the morning, but they all struggle with the evening.

It is worth carrying out an energy audit occasionally to help you understand when you are the most energetic and effective. One of my friends claims to be both an 'Owl' and a 'Lark' but they can't do much in between!

'Digital Native' or 'Digital Immigrant'

My sixth preference pair considers how someone approaches technology. 'Digital Natives' have grown up with digital technology. They do not know a time when there has not been digital technology, whereas 'Digital Immigrants' have adapted and adopted digital technology.

When telephones were something that had to be wired into a box on your wall, a very flashy friend of mine turned up with his mobile telephone. The word ‘mobile’ may have been an overstatement, as the handset was attached to something like a car battery! But it was one of the first mobile phones, so I am someone who remembers life before digital technology.

I never forget the day when one of my children as a toddler walked over to the TV screen and tried to change channel by swiping the screen. When it didn’t work they said, “Daddy it’s broken”!

I remember the days before the Internet, whereas my kids are rather astonished to think that there were such days; they are definitely ‘Digital Natives’. Are you a ‘Digital Immigrant’ or are you a ‘Digital Native’?

These are just six preference pairs, of many others you can identify. Through the Relationology Academy people have suggested other preferences such as ‘Diplomatic’ and ‘Direct’ to understand people’s softness and candour; or ‘Entrepreneurs’ and ‘Operations People’ to differentiate their tendency to pioneer and build.

It is also important to remember that preference pairs present options that are not right, not wrong... just different. People are hardwired and that is their natural preference for dealing with life.

Being able to engage with the different types of individuals helps you become a better leader.

Understanding preferences

Research from Gallup shows that 70 per cent of engagement is determined by team leaders and managers and how they truly understand the preferences of people in their teams. Each person is unique and if managers and team leaders can create ways of engaging people then discretionary effort and motivation follow. Their team outperforms others because they are being their true selves. When you help other people to be authentic they perform at their very best.

Leaders of high-performance teams have to learn the art of being ambidextrous. They need to learn to adapt to people, by understanding their preferences and regulating their approach and interactions with them to achieve the very best result.

Matt's Mission

***My mission for you is to work out the preference profiles for at least two other people you work with, or maybe a whole team, and draw a grid*.**

Write their names and work out what preferences they have and the way they like to work.

For each of those people, make commitments to how you are going to engage with them, in a way that matches their preferences. Do not force your preferences upon others and expect them to dance to your drumbeat.

If you accept my mission, you will enable other people to be authentically who they are and support them in achieving even greater results.

LEADING HIGH PERFORMANCE TEAMS

Preferences		Person
Introvert	Extrovert	
Left	Right	
Project	People	
Earlybird	Lastminute	
Owl	Lark	
Native	Immigrant	

SuperPower #6
Building Networks, Forums & Communities

After being asked by a high street bank to design and deliver a learning and development programme for their staff, I eagerly started work on a proposal. The procurement process was rather painful, I remember, and it was staggering how much paperwork needed putting into place. Eventually, after organising many policies and insurances, I finally submitted my proposal.

It was rather exciting when I discovered that my bid had been successful. Just a few days before I began to deliver the programme, the HR director telephoned me to tell me what they *really* needed! I was somewhat surprised at this. He went on to explain that the bank had undergone continuous restructuring and reshaping.

The result of these continuous changes meant the bank needed to develop relationships, community and trust. He asked me to put everything I had designed to one side to focus on this important task.

Of course, I was more than happy to agree. Relationships, community and trust are my core passion and transformational in any environment.

A community built from scratch

Just over 150 miles south of Rome there is a small town called Roseto in the Abruzzo region of central Italy. In

1882, 11 residents left the community and emigrated to the United States. They spent their first night sleeping on the floor of a mill in New York before heading out to Pennsylvania, where they found an area that they decided to make their own. From that day, they started building a community from scratch.

Year after year, more Rosetans travelled from Italy to make their new home in the United States. As dozens of people made the long journey across the Atlantic, more followed them after hearing how good their new life was.

This new community was named Roseto, Pennsylvania, and a professor, Dr Stuart Wolf, became intrigued by the community while on holiday nearby. While chatting with a couple of residents in a local bar, Dr Wolf was fascinated not only by their town – which they built from scratch – but how there was virtually no chronic heart disease in people under the age of 65.

Dr Wolf decided to carry out comprehensive research and began looking at the diet of the Rosetans, thinking there was something particular about what they ate. They then turned their attentions to the climate and wondered if that was the key before moving on to looking at their genetics. Everything that the research team investigated appeared to have no effect on the healthy hearts of the Rosetans.

After extensive analysis Dr Wolf and his team came to a remarkable conclusion. The community that built the relationships and the trust within the community was transformative to people's health.

The Harvard Study of Adult Development is the longest longitudinal study in history and spans more than eight decades. The third director of studies concluded that the quality of a person's relationships at 50 years old, was the best indicator of their health when they reached the age of 80.

Now, I'm not suggesting you should eat and drink whatever you like, as long as you have great relationships to guarantee a long life! But it is clear that the biggest factor in this research was the quality of the human relationships of those people.

Community and wellness

Professor Julianne Holt-Lunstad, from Brigham Young University, led a project called Social Relationships on Mortality Risk and surmised that people who were exposed to prolonged periods of social isolation, had a 50 per cent higher death rate.

Not only do relationships and community create better well-being and wellness, but also longevity of life. The benefits of community, of networks and of forums are incredibly powerful.

I have built networks, forums and communities in the business world, the public sector and the non-profit sector in the UK and around the world. And everything I have learned from this process has helped me develop a 7-step model: it's a circle with seven segments – or perhaps a cake with seven slices – going around clockwise.

Building a community

The first step to building a community or a network or a forum, which I sum up as communities, is to identify a human need. What is it that people need? A community built around a genuine human need has a purpose.

What is interesting is that pain is twice as motivating as opportunity. I can offer you an opportunity, which you may or may not take. But if I can relieve you of pain, you will be eager to grab the chance with both hands. In identifying human need, we're identifying the motivation for people to be involved. So step one of building a community is to identify need.

Define goals

Whenever I start a new venture or build a community, a network or a forum, I like to pick three goals. I like the first goal to be easily achievable because it's like low-hanging fruit – it's what you pick first because it's easily achievable. A short-term goal that is simple to complete creates a sense of confidence.

The second goal needs to be more challenging and a medium-term aim, while the third goal is longer-term and super ambitious. Setting goals is an essential second step.

Focus on influencers

In every sector there are key influencers, leaders of leaders and gatekeepers. By getting these people in the room, most others will follow.

Whenever I start a new community, I consider those individuals I can win over first. By doing this, you can leverage other people into the room – and it works every time! Engage the strategic stakeholders and everyone else will follow.

Arrange a meeting

The fourth step is quite simply to arrange a meeting. But before rushing headlong, carefully consider the venue, time, and make sure the date suits as many people as possible. It is imperative to ensure that the date suits the influencers who others will follow.

Putting in a lot of effort to contact those key to the meeting is essential to ensure as many influencers as possible are in attendance. Remember that the first meeting creates the benchmark for everything else that happens thereafter.

Formulate the network

The fifth step is to formulate the network; which is to give the community, network or forum a name. There are times when I don't immediately give a network its name. Sometimes, I allow it to meet three or four times before naming it.

My reason for not always networks immediately is if there are strong political forces at play. That may sound strange, but the more political a community, network or forum is, the better it is to delay the handle. Naming the network too soon can be divisive as it can feel like you are making too much of a political play.

I encourage you to meet, formulate and then give your network a name and then of course create an online presence. When your community, network or forum has an online presence it is real. Nothing exists without a website and social media.

Grow the community

Once you have formulated and given your community a name, the sixth step is to grow the community. By following the previous five steps, the community should grow naturally, incrementally and relatively easily. If you have identified a need, set some goals, engaged key influencers, held a meeting, named your network and created an online presence, anyone who empathises with you will want to be part of the growth.

Focus on achievements

No one wants to be part of a talking shop, they want to be part of something that does things and has achievements under its belt. At this stage, it is important to work your way through the goals, including short-term, medium-term and long-term. Once you accomplish these goals, set new ones.

Always establish the fact that you are achieving and doing something because as long as you are achieving, the key influencers and other participants will want to continue to be a part of the network.

These are the seven steps I continue to use whenever I set up a community, and I can assure you that they work.

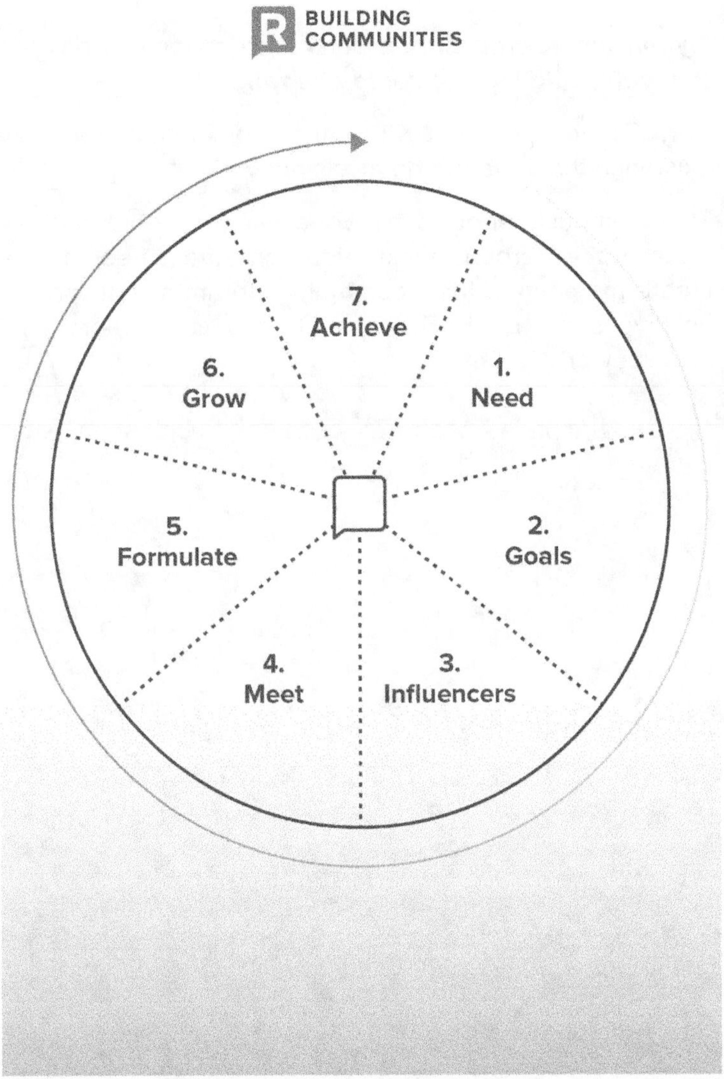
BUILDING
COMMUNITIES
7.
Achieve
1.
Need
2.
Goals
3.
Influencers
4.
Meet
5.
Formulate
6.
Grow

Matt's Mission

My mission for this SuperPower is to choose a network that you could start or could strengthen.

Don't run too quickly to strengthen something already in existence that is someone else's network.

Think seriously about a network that you could start. Is there a need around which you can attract people and create momentum for a community, forum or network to achieve some goals? Because this is an extraordinary superpower!

SuperPower #7
Differentiating Yourself

In pretty much every business sector, there is a crowded and saturated marketplace. Sometimes it can seem like an insurmountable challenge to gain a foothold let alone a competitive advantage. But there is an answer, and that is, of course, your relationships.

Looking back through my life, I can honestly say that the most amazing, memorable and transformational events that happened were the result of relationships.

As a teenager, I used to cycle around the neighbourhood at the weekend and wash people's cars; and I remember on one occasion, after being paid for my work, a gentleman asked what I was going to do when leaving school. I answered that I had lots of ideas but wasn't exactly sure of my next step.

The next time I arrived to wash his car, the man handed me an application form for a job he thought I might be interested in. After helping me with the application, I was fortunate to be called for an interview and the man helped me with interview technique... to cut a long story short, I got the job. It was where my career began – and all thanks to the chap with the dirty car!

Differentiate yourself

During a chat with a friend, our conversation turned to a leadership conference where I was to be the keynote speaker. After I revealed my topic of relationships and how I was going to present it, he said sharply to me, "Matt, that's a book!"

To be honest, I was somewhat taken aback when my friend, who had written many books himself, made this suggestion. But that was nothing compared to my astonishment moments later when he reached for his phone to call his editor.

I sat there rather bewildered as he began to talk to the person at the other end of the phone: "I've got this guy here with me and he's got a book in him, will you publish it?"

As he passed me the telephone, I almost wet myself! That's where my first book began. What differentiated my connection with the publisher compared to the hundreds of manuscripts they would receive a year – a relationship.

In SuperPower 3, I recall the time when the senior partner of a firm I worked with announced to me that he was about to retire. After congratulating him, I raised the question about who I needed to deal with in the future. In response, the retiring partner suggested I host one of my cheese and wine evenings. From there, I developed a relationship with one of the partners, and that led to me securing my first blue chip contract.

Actions like these are what differentiate you in a crowded, saturated, competitive marketplace. It's thanks to the relationships that you become known, liked and trusted.

The Plus One Strategy

Like anything in business, the way to move forward successfully is to develop a strategy; and I want to share with you my strategy and approach for differentiating yourself by building an ecosystem of relationships.

I don't know if you have a relationship strategy, but don't worry if you haven't as most people don't either. I would love to share with you my relationship strategy, which is my gift from me to you.

My strategy is to collect, keep and grow relationships. It sounds easy, but some people are completely overwhelmed by the number of people they know. Others, however, are desperate to find new connections, especially when life is going through change. They may have moved country, house or job, whatever it might be, they want to connect with new people.

There is huge value in continuously collecting new relationships. I have discovered that the effective approach is to build them one at a time, which may sound incredibly simple. Whether I go to an event, online or offline, I am alert to those in attendance to discern one person I can have a profound and meaningful connection with. Who is the one person I could add to my ecosystem of relationships and who would like to add me to theirs? And so I follow what I call the Plus One Strategy.

Introverts generally do not enjoy the thought of going into a crowded room, whether that is a physical one or an online meeting. But, to those, I suggest you forget about meeting loads of people. What's most important is connecting to *one* other person to have a meaningful, profound connection with.

I have been to events where some people are flitting between attendees doling out business cards like there's no tomorrow in the hope of increasing their contact book. But that strategy is, more often than not, likely to completely fail.

My strategy for collecting relationships is to focus on finding a connection with one person at a time.

Keep relationships

The second step of the strategy is to keep your relationships. As I have mentioned, we have all seen the business person who dishes out business cards like they're going to be past their sell-by date. Now, it is perfectly reasonable to collect business cards, but it's what you do with them after the meeting has ended that matters.

Unless you follow through on the people you meet, you might as well have stayed at home or not bothered logging into the video event. I have a commitment that within 24 hours I will follow-up with anyone that I've met that I want to keep in contact with.

And this is where I introduce for the second time, the Pareto principle; or the 80/20 rule as it is often known. If you apply this principle, then you will put 80 per cent of your time, energy and resources into 20 per cent of your relationships. But always keep 20 per cent of your time, energy and resources available to invest in the relationships you haven't prioritised.

Make sure that you always have something to give to people, even if is very small. To keep your relational ecosystem alive look for legitimate reasons to be in contact with the people you know. Maybe they have been promoted, received some bad news or perhaps it is their birthday or wedding anniversary – use every opportunity available to you to keep in contact with people.

It's especially important to build relationships with people before you need something from them – every positive contact you have with them is a deposit in the trust account you have with each other.

Should your relationships just become transactional people can feel used and abused, to the detriment of the relationship. The authentic way to show how much we genuinely care and value people in our ecosystem is by keeping in contact with them when we don't want anything from them.

Grow relationships

After collecting and keeping relationships, the next step is to focus on growing relationships. There will always be those few relationships that are deeper due to various factors, such as geography. It is easier to keep in touch with those we live close to. Or you may be working on a project together so you are in constant contact.

The result of such relationships is that you grow deep trust. As I mentioned in SuperPower 3, research by Professor Mark Granovetter, from Stanford University, showed that 56 per cent of people were in their current job through a relationship they had that made a way for them into that current position.

And through my work with the recruitment industry, I have often been told that two-thirds of jobs are never advertised because they go to people known by the employer. Both of these statistics prove that opportunities for growth come from relationships, that is, the people we already know.

Be proactive

My three-step strategy is incredibly effective, but my advice to you is to use it and be proactive, deliberate and intentional. Most people are rather passive about relationships. You can give out 100 business cards but, typically you will hear from less than a handful of them again. It doesn't matter how many business cards you give out, it's the ones you collect that matter because those are the ones you can follow through on.

You can differentiate yourself immediately in your marketplace by adopting my relationship strategy and being intentional, deliberate and proactive. You immediately set yourself apart and differentiate yourself from the majority of people because you are proactive about collecting, keeping and growing relationships.

I would be the first to admit that some of us are better at collecting than keeping and some are better at keeping than collecting. Introverts are generally better at keeping relationships, for example. They prefer, for all sorts of reasons, not to meet lots of new people all at once. But they excel at relationships with the people they know.

By contrast, the extroverts tend to be better at collecting relationships. They're great at walking into crowded rooms or joining online meetings and connecting with lots of people. The extroverts, however, are more likely to be poor at keeping in contact with all the people they already know.

It is a genuine SuperPower to learn to both collect and keep and keep and collect, in a sense you need to become ambidextrous about your relationships.

Six months into my marriage, my wife, Esther, sat me down one weekend and asked, "Do we have to invite someone different for dinner every night at the weekend?" I looked at her and felt somewhat puzzled because I had never considered it a problem.

Then she asked, "Do you think we could invite the same people more than once?"

This is the classic behaviour of an introvert and an extrovert! Through the challenge of my wife, I have learned to work just as hard at keeping relationships as I do collecting them.

Matt's Mission

My final mission, should you choose to accept it, is a choice of two challenges.

For all those who are great at collecting relationships, reach out to three people that you have met historically but haven't been in contact with for a long time. Ensure that you reach out now before you want something from them. Check to see how they are and work intentionally at keeping those relationships.

If, on the other hand, you are good at keeping relationships but do not excel at collecting and nurturing them, I would like to challenge you to set yourself a target of how many new relationships you're going to add to your ecosystem on a regular basis.

By accepting the mission, people who are collecting relationships can become better at keeping them and those who are best at keeping relationships can become better collectors. We will become ambidextrous.

As a result, this will help you move from being ordinary to becoming extraordinary in your relationships.

DIFFERENTIATING YOURSELF

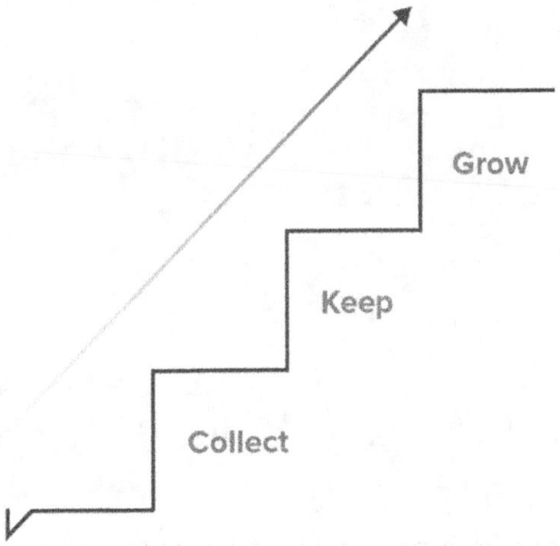

Conclusion

When it comes to your enterprise, investment is necessary throughout its lifespan or you risk being out of touch, outdated and out of business. Whether that is through financing materials, staff training, research and development or marketing... you really do get out what you put in.

As these 7 SuperPowers show, investment in relationships is an area you cannot ignore. With many different types of relationships, it can seem extremely daunting and sometimes impossible to invest your time, especially if you know a lot of people.

But introducing SuperPowers to your life will not only give you opportunities to invest and manage your relationships, it can lead to tangible growth both in you and your business or enterprise.

Please remember to revisit the infographics as they offer an effective visual aid that will help you implement the SuperPowers to your relationships. Building your relational ecosystem will become a beneficial addition to your business strategy and a wise investment that will reap dividends.

You may be overawed by some of the Matt's Missions and may not wish to accept them. But can I encourage you to work even harder at those that feel out of your comfort zone? To be challenged leads to successful growth, and I hope that you will be able to accept even the toughest missions for you.

My belief is that relationships are the true currency of business, so invest in your relationships and your SuperPowers and not only will those within your ecosystem profit, you will too. They are worthy of more investment from every one of us!

About the Author

Matt Bird is a business and social entrepreneur, a global speaker, author and broadcaster.

He has spoken in 50 countries to more than a million people, authored 17 books and writes for publications such as The Times newspaper.

Matt has pioneered numerous social and business ventures which currently include:

- NAYBA, a global foundation helping local churches love their neighbours and transform their neighbourhoods, where he is the Founder.
- PublishU, a global venture helping people write, publish and market their books worldwide, where he is the Chief Coach.
- Relationology, a global community of great people doing great things through great relationships, where he is the founding Partner.
- Noto Italy, a venture helping people rest and invest in the city of Noto in Sicily, Italy.
- Matt-Bird.com, a platform inspiring people in faith through his speaking, writing and broadcasting.

When he is not travelling he lives between London, United Kingdom and Noto, Italy.

www.CoffeeWithMatt.com

About the Author

About Relationology International

Relationology International helps leaders and their organisations build profitable relationships.

- The **Relationology Academy** for private clients provides masterminds and courses that enable leaders to acquire new skills and relationships in order to achieve new success.
- The **Relationology Consulting** for corporate clients delivers bespoke learning and development programmes that enable people to become more effective in building client and collegiate relationships.
- The **Relationology Coaching** for executives who want to achieve higher levels of personal performance and business impact.

Relationology corporate and executive clients include PwC International, UK Home Office, Investec Bank South Africa and the US Federal Reserve Bank.

www.relationologyinternational.com

Other Books

Relationology 101
Grow Your Business
Building Profitable Relationships
SuperPowers

www.PublishU.com

www.ingramcontent.com/pod-product-compliance
Lightning Source LLC
Chambersburg PA
CBHW070920220526
45467CB00004B/1485
* 9 7 9 8 7 1 3 6 5 2 5 7 9 *